THE BEST BOOK OF

Gymnastics

Christine Morley

KINGFISHER

BOSTON

Contents

KINGFISHER

a Houghton Mifflin Company imprint
222 Berkeley Street
Boston, Massachusetts 02116

www.houghtonmifflinbooks.com

Created for Kingfisher Publications by
Picthall & Gunzi Limited

Author: Christine Morley
Designer: Dominic Zwemmer
Editors: Christiane Gunzi and
Lauren Robertson
Illustrator: Michael White
Consultant: Lloyd Readhead

First published by Kingfisher
Publications Plc 2003

10 9 8 7 6 5 4 3 2 1

1TR/0403/WKT/MAR(MAR)/128/KMA

ISBN 0-7534-5605-2

Printed in China

4 What is gymnastics?

6 The first gymnasts

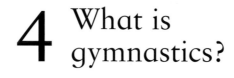

14 Amazing balance

16 All types of shapes

24 Skillful somersaults

26 Working as a team

8 Getting ready

10 On the mat

12 Jumps and leaps

18 High up in the air

20 On the horse

22 Music and dance

28 Watching displays

30 Gymnastic events

31 Glossary
32 Index

What is gymnastics?

Gymnastics is an enjoyable sport that keeps the body in shape. It is done by gymnasts who perform special movements and shapes that link together to make a routine. Gymnastics is divided into disciplines, or styles, including artistic gymnastics, sports acrobatics, trampolining, tumbling, and rhythmic gymnastics. Gymnastics is done on a floor mat or on equipment such as the balance beam or vault. Enthusiastic gymnasts can enter competitions.

Pair of sports acrobatic gymnasts performing a balance position

In floor work girls and boys train on their own on a padded floor mat.

The pommel horse is used for swings, circles, and scissor movements.

The parallel bars are used only by male gymnasts.

4

Rhythmic gymnastics is set to music, and gymnasts use small hand apparatus such as the ball.

The rings are used in boys' and men's artistic gymnastics.

The horizontal bar is a piece of equipment used only by men.

The uneven bars are used by women and girls for swings, circles, and handstand positions.

The balance beam is used by women. It is only 4 in. wide, but experienced gymnasts can leap, jump, and somersault on it.

The vaulting horse has a nonslip, padded surface that makes it soft and springy.

5

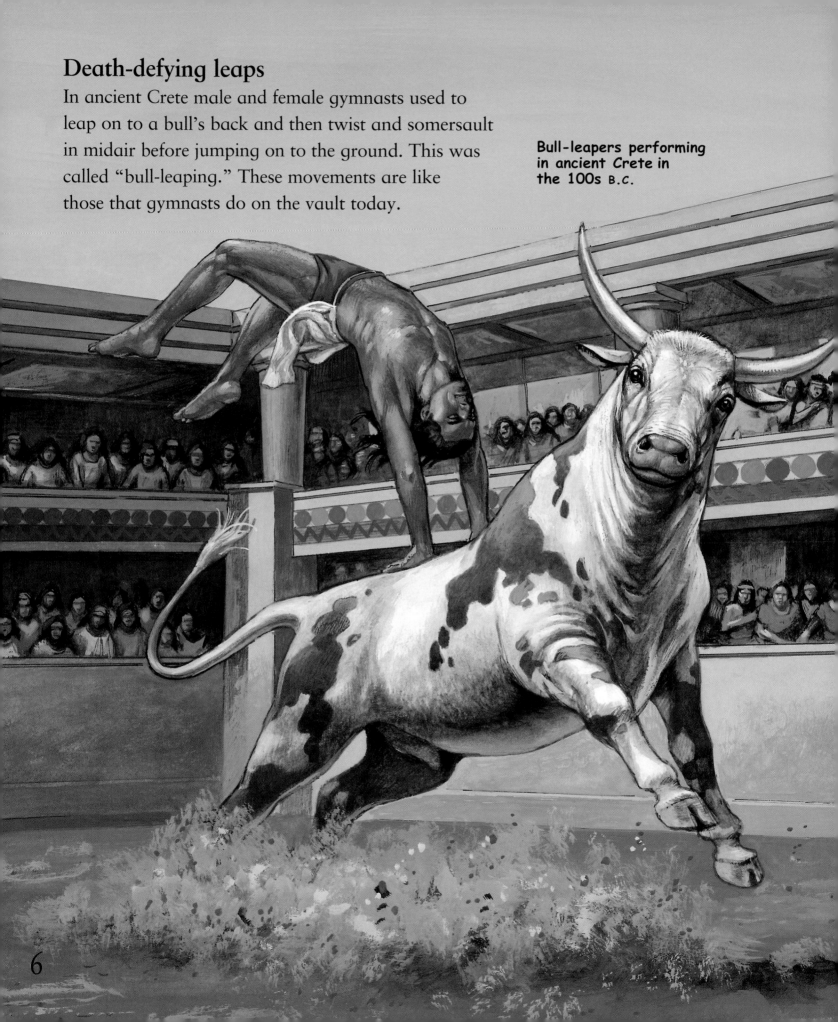

Death-defying leaps

In ancient Crete male and female gymnasts used to leap on to a bull's back and then twist and somersault in midair before jumping on to the ground. This was called "bull-leaping." These movements are like those that gymnasts do on the vault today.

Bull-leapers performing in ancient Crete in the 100s B.C.

6

The first gymnasts

Gymnastics has been performed since early times. In 3000 B.C. the ancient Egyptians did vaults and floor exercises, and the ancient Greeks held tumbling competitions. Soldiers in ancient China were taught gymnastics as part of their training. When these very old civilizations died out, gymnastics did, too. It became popular again in the 1800s.

Medieval acrobatic performers

17th-century acrobatics display

Traveling acrobats

In medieval Europe gymnastics was practiced by traveling performers. They went from town to town and entertained people with acrobatics, songs, juggling, and tricks.

A spectator sport

During the 1600s entertainers performed acrobatics at the royal courts. They would also perform on stage during intermissions of plays to keep the audience amused.

Getting ready

Many girls and boys learn gymnastics at school where it is taught in gym class. If you are interested in doing gymnastics, you can join a club at a local gym or train for competitions with your school. You can ask about the different types of gymnastics and decide which type is best for you. General gymnastics includes skills from all of the different styles. Or you may want to learn a particular type of gymnastics such as trampolining.

Finding a coach

Sports clubs often give lessons for beginners. Before choosing a coach or gym club go along with an adult and watch a class to see if it is right for you.

Instructor and pupils doing a warm-up

Side stretches to work muscles in body and legs

What to wear

As a beginner you can wear shorts and a T-shirt. For competitions gymnasts wear leotards, which are stretchy and tight fitting and allow them to move easily. When boys work on the bars or rings, they wear sweatpants.

Warming up

Training sessions start with a 10–20 minute warm-up to stretch the muscles. It is important to do a warm-up because if you do not, you could injure your muscles and joints.

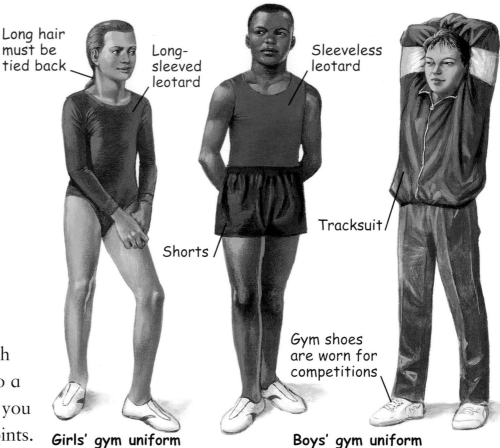

Long hair must be tied back

Long-sleeved leotard

Sleeveless leotard

Shorts

Tracksuit

Gym shoes are worn for competitions

Girls' gym uniform

Boys' gym uniform

Forward bends to loosen muscles in backs of legs

9

On the mat

Foam mat for all types of floor work

Springboard for extra lift when jumping

Wedge mat helps move body weight when rolling

Artistic gymnastics is fascinating to watch. The girls work on the vault, uneven bars, balance beam, and floor. The boys use the floor, pommels, rings, vault, parallel bars, and horizontal bar. The floor routines include acrobatic and tumbling movements, as well as jumps, leaps, and exercises. These moves show flexibility and strength. Traditionally girls' routines are set to music and include dance moves. Boys' exercises include stronger movements and stunning acrobatics.

Equipment

Floor work takes place on a thick foam mat. It is springy and soft to land on. Sloped wedges of foam are used to help beginners learn rolls. Springboards are for mounting the vault, balance beam, and bars.

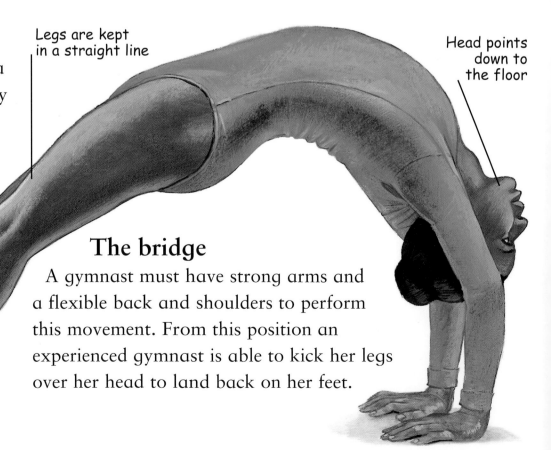

Legs are kept in a straight line

Head points down to the floor

Feet are pressed firmly into the floor

The bridge

A gymnast must have strong arms and a flexible back and shoulders to perform this movement. From this position an experienced gymnast is able to kick her legs over her head to land back on her feet.

Forward roll

Rolling is useful for linking one movement to another. It is best to practice this on a soft mat. The gymnast starts in a squatting position with the arms stretched forward and the back straight.

Gymnast leans forward and puts hands on sides of head to take body weight, tucking in head.

Gymnast gives a push with feet, rolls forward, and then comes back into a squatting position.

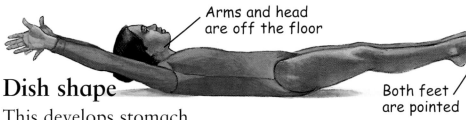

Arms and head
are off the floor

Both feet
are pointed

Dish shape

This develops stomach and leg muscles and helps improve posture. The lower back is pressed into the floor. The shoulders, arms, and legs are lifted a few inches off the ground.

Handstand

In order to do a handstand well a gymnast's body has to stay straight and still. With enough training a gymnast can perform handstands on the vault, balance beam, rings, and bars.

Handstand on bar

Box split

In a box split the back is straight, and the legs are stretched wide to form a straight line. It takes a lot of practice to make the hips and legs flexible enough to do this.

Arms can be stretched
out wide or above the head

Box split on floor

Knees turn upward,
and toes are pointed

11

2 After doing a somersault in midair the gymnast straightens her body to prepare for landing.

Hands are stretched out

1 As the gymnast dismounts from the uneven bars she builds up enough speed and power to somersault high up in the air.

Body is straight

A difficult dismount means that the judges will give more points.

3 The gymnast holds her arms out wide to control her landing. When she lands, her knees must bend.

Toes are pointed

Jumps and leaps

Gymnasts perform all types of breathtaking leaps and jumps on the mat and on equipment. They are able to make amazing shapes with their bodies in midair. Using jumps and leaps gymnasts link these shapes together to impress the judges with their power and style. A jump means taking off on two feet and landing on two feet. A leap is when the gymnast takes off on one foot but lands on the other foot.

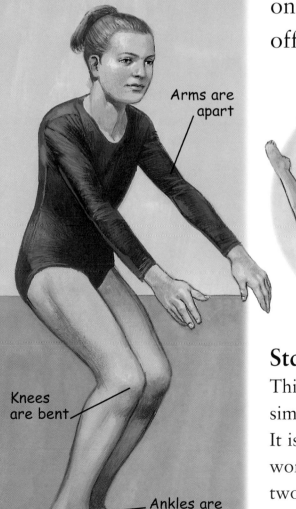

4 As the gymnast lands she must not wobble or take any extra steps. If she does, she will lose points.

Arms are apart

Knees are bent

Ankles are together

Stag leap
This dramatic shape looks similar to a running stag. It is used in floor and beam work. You can jump from two feet or take one or two steps forward and then leap.

Straddle pike jump
A gymnast has to jump up high in order to have enough time to make this difficult shape. It is usually performed on the trampoline and sometimes as a floor exercise.

Amazing balance

To perform balancing positions, such as headstands and handstands, gymnasts need to be strong and able to concentrate very hard. Beginners learn to balance on the floor with simple exercises such as raising one leg and holding it still for ten seconds. To learn how to work on the balance beam gymnasts train along a line drawn on the floor, and then they move on to a low balance beam. They gradually work on higher levels until they reach a balance beam that is about four feet off the ground.

Arabesque is a balancing position performed on the floor.

1 In an arabesque the gymnast starts with her arms raised behind her head, making a strong outline with her body.

2 Then the gymnast lifts one leg backward and points her toes. At the same time she begins bringing both of her arms forward.

3 She leans her weight on to her front leg and lifts up her free leg behind her. She lifts up her head and stretches out her arms.

On the balance beam

Balancing on a beam is difficult, and any
wobbling is marked down by the judges.
Gymnasts must know where to place their feet
without looking down. This gymnast shows
strength, suppleness, and balance by making
the shape of the letter "Y" with her body.

The gymnast's
supporting leg
and foot are
very strong.

Balance beam is
only 14 in. wide

15

All types of shapes

The shapes that gymnasts make with their bodies must look as attractive as possible. Some shapes, such as the dish, are fairly easy to do. Others, such as the bridge, take a lot of practice to perform well. In order to learn how to do a shape accurately gymnasts can sometimes need the help of a "spotter," who guides and supports them through the movement. To do the back walkover the gymnast below needs a flexible back and hips.

Toes are pointed

Arms are held out straight

Supporting foot presses into floor

Back walkover on floor

1 The gymnast begins by lifting her right leg out in front of her. She keeps her back straight and her arms stretched up above her head.

2 She reaches backward, and her hips move forward. During practice a spotter supports the gymnast as she leans back.

3 Placing her hands on the floor she points her fingers toward her feet. Her left leg is slightly bent, and her right leg points up.

16

Tight twist

The Yurchenko full twist is named after the gymnast Natalie Yurchenko, who perfected this move. Champions will often perform movements with at least one twist.

High handstand

Gymnasts need strength and balance to do a handstand on the parallel bars and rings. They must hold the position for at least two seconds. This male gymnast is practicing on parallettes.

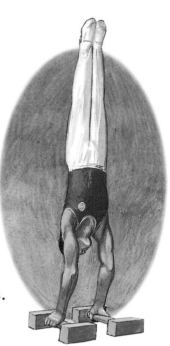

A split-legs handstand

Leg is brought down smoothly

Gymnast keeps an extended body shape

4 The gymnast shifts her weight on to her hands as she pushes up with her left leg. She brings her right leg down toward the floor.

5 As the gymnast's right leg reaches the floor her left leg keeps moving back. Her toes must be pointed at all times.

6 When both of her feet are back on the ground, the gymnast stands up tall, raises her arms, points her hands back, and smiles!

The cross

Only male gymnasts use the rings. Their ring routines must include swinging exercises with at least two handstands. This advanced position is called the cross. A beginner can practice this if a spotter holds his ankles and supports his weight.

Legs are held in straight line and kept close together

High up in the air

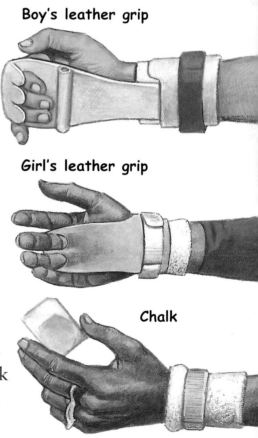

The most dramatic movements are performed high up in the air on the rings and the bars. Female gymnasts use the uneven bars, and male gymnasts work on the parallel bars and the horizontal bar. They perform moves such as somersaults, swings, and twists. They also do release and catch moves. Gymnasts' dismounts are always spectacular to watch.

Handstand

The handstand is a difficult position that takes a lot of strength. In order to perform it correctly the gymnast must keep his ankles, knees, hips, and shoulders in a straight line.

Protecting the hands

Gymnasts often wear grips, or handguards, to stop their hands from getting sore. The grips fit over the fingers and fasten around the wrists. Gymnasts also use chalk to soak up sweat from their hands and feet so that they do not slip.

Handstand

Boy's leather grip

Girl's leather grip

Chalk

19

On the horse

In gymnastics "horses" are pieces of equipment that gymnasts jump over. Long ago they were shaped like real horses, with a head and neck, but they do not look like that today. In competitions gymnasts use padded platforms—either a vaulting horse or a vaulting table. The pommel is another type of horse. The horses are all soft and springy.

Body is straight as gymnast springs upward

Body stays straight as gymnast flies forward

Gymnast jumps up high from springboard

Hands are placed on horse for handstand

Handspring vault

The handspring vault is a moderately advanced move for boys and girls. With enough height and speed experienced gymnasts can jump through the air, land on their hands on the vault, and then spring off and land upright on their feet again.

The pommel horse

The pommel horse stands 45 in. high. It is very difficult to use and needs a lot of concentration and strength. The gymnast must swing his body across and around the horse while balancing on one hand. His legs should never touch the pommel horse.

Male gymnast using pommel horse

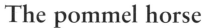

Legs are kept together with toes pointed

Other gymnasts waiting for their turn to perform

Knees are bent

Body and legs are straight

21

Music and dance

One of the most graceful types of gymnastics is rhythmic gymnastics, performed by girls and women. Dance or balletlike moves are done to music while the gymnasts use pieces of hand apparatus such as ribbons and hoops. Rhythmic gymnasts work with the music and bring their own style to the routine.

Using ribbons and hoops

Rhythmic gymnasts work on their own or in groups of up to six people. Girls in the group can use different hand apparatus, which they pass, throw, and roll to each other. In a group competition the gymnasts have between two-and-a-half and three minutes to complete the routine.

This gymnast can make beautiful shapes with the ribbon, but it should not touch her body or get tangled.

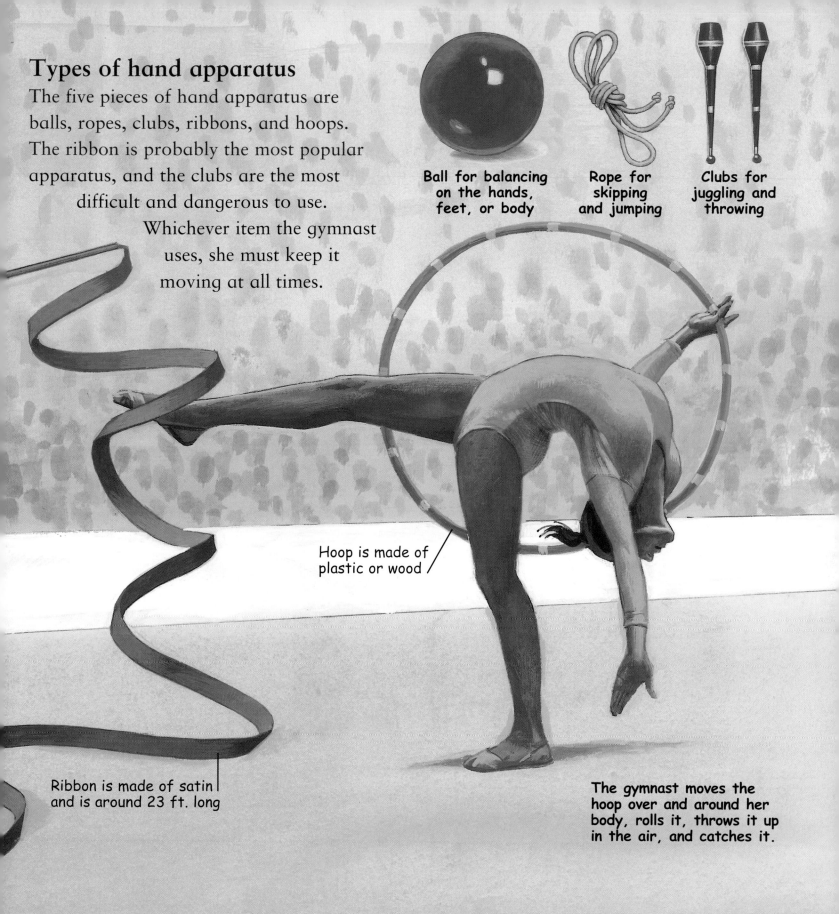

Types of hand apparatus

The five pieces of hand apparatus are balls, ropes, clubs, ribbons, and hoops. The ribbon is probably the most popular apparatus, and the clubs are the most difficult and dangerous to use. Whichever item the gymnast uses, she must keep it moving at all times.

Ball for balancing on the hands, feet, or body

Rope for skipping and jumping

Clubs for juggling and throwing

Hoop is made of plastic or wood

Ribbon is made of satin and is around 23 ft. long

The gymnast moves the hoop over and around her body, rolls it, throws it up in the air, and catches it.

Trampoline training

Gymnasts spend hours on the trampoline practicing their routines. They use the same basic movements and somersaults as those used in artistic gymnastics. A coach corrects any mistakes.

Coach giving instructions

Gymnast stays as high as she can when performing moves

Skillful somersaults

Spotters standing on each side to make sure gymnast does not fall off trampoline

In trampolining gymnasts do daring movements such as very high somersaults. In Sydney, Australia, in 2000 this became an Olympic sport. Tumbling is an older sport and is also exciting to watch. Gymnasts run along a track to build up speed and then do a series of somersaults and twists in just six seconds. It takes years of hard work for a gymnast to perform for just a few thrilling seconds.

Terrific tumblers

In 1932 tumbling was an Olympic sport. It is no longer an Olympic sport, but gymnasts can still enter championships. In competitions they perform three runs, showing twists, somersaults, and a combination of both. The best tumblers can do three double somersaults plus twists in a single run!

25

Working as a team

Sports acrobatics is a type of gymnastics that developed from acrobatic circus displays. It involves balance and tumbling skills. Girls and boys do routines on floor mats in pairs or in threes and fours. There are balance exercises to do and also exercises called "tempo." Tempo is where one gymnast performs somersaults, twists, and turns while being thrown into the air by her partner.

Triple balance

Girls perform balances in pairs or in groups of three. Here they are doing a dramatic triple balance.

The judges give marks for strength, steadiness, and style. In competitions each balance must be held for at least two seconds.

The legs can be straight or bent.

The back and arms must be straight.

"Top" rests hands on knees of "base" to keep arms steady.

"Base" has back and feet in stable position.

Working in pairs

When gymnasts work together in pairs, the person who is supporting the weight is called the "base," and the person who is being supported is called the "top." This pair of gymnasts is performing the shoulder balance.

26

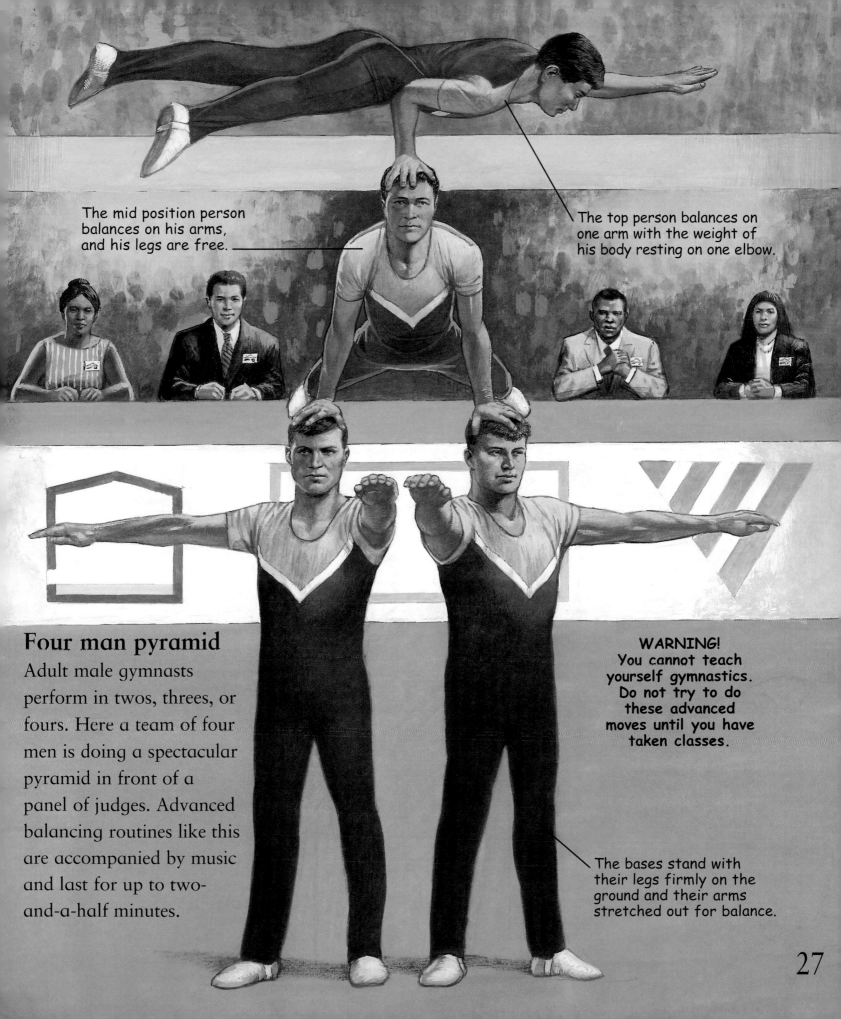

The mid position person balances on his arms, and his legs are free.

The top person balances on one arm with the weight of his body resting on one elbow.

Four man pyramid

Adult male gymnasts perform in twos, threes, or fours. Here a team of four men is doing a spectacular pyramid in front of a panel of judges. Advanced balancing routines like this are accompanied by music and last for up to two-and-a-half minutes.

WARNING!
You cannot teach yourself gymnastics. Do not try to do these advanced moves until you have taken classes.

The bases stand with their legs firmly on the ground and their arms stretched out for balance.

27

Watching displays

There are many opportunities to see gymnastic displays. You can watch competitions between schools and clubs or go to events such as championships. Major events, including the Olympics, are shown on TV. You can also watch gymnastics at the circus. The famous Chinese State Circus tours the world with its daring teams of acrobats and balance artists.

Champion acrobats

Acrobatic displays have been practiced in China for more than 2,000 years. The Chinese State Circus acrobats use objects, such as chairs and hoops, to perform incredible feats of strength and balance. These are very exciting to watch.

Acrobats forming a human pyramid

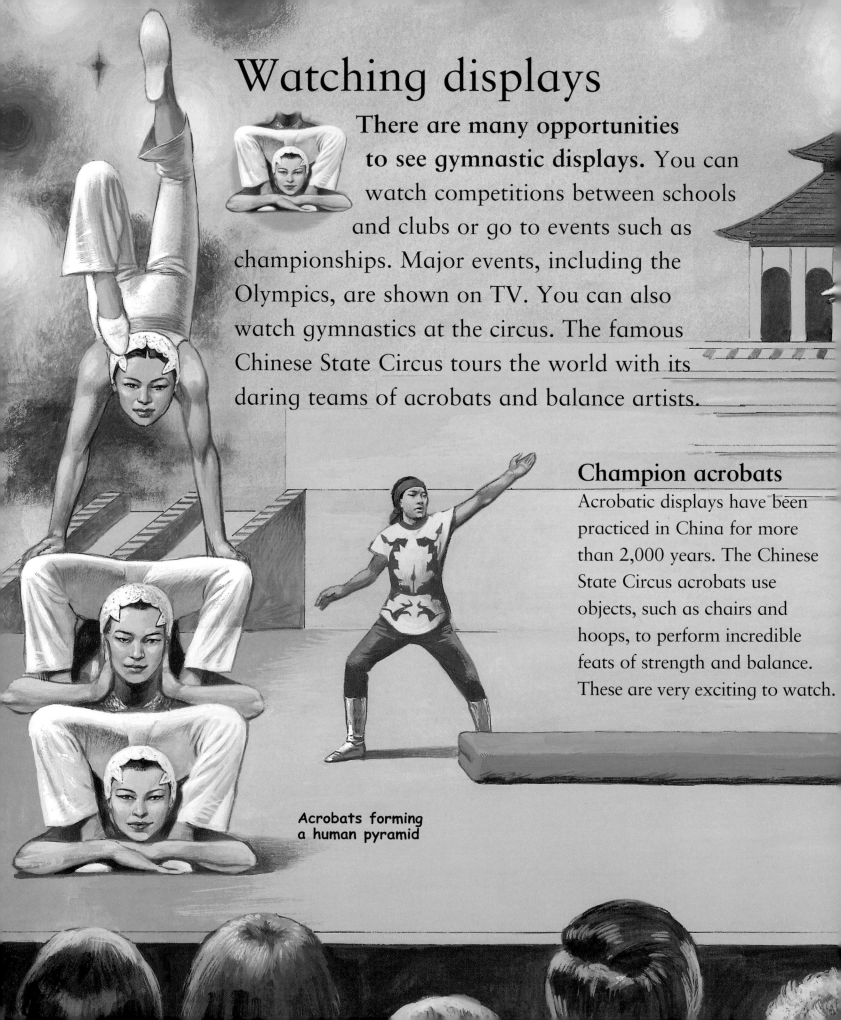

Cheerleaders performing a balancing act

Ra ra ra!

Cheerleaders entertain crowds at football games in the U.S. They chant rhymes to their team while they do leaps, splits, and balances with props such as batons.

Acrobat doing a high back flip through hoop

Acrobat balancing on a pole using only one hand

Gymnastics events

Modern gymnastics competitions have been held for more than one hundred years. The biggest events are the Olympic Games and the World Championships. There are also competitions between clubs and schools, with events for all ages and levels. Even if you are not competing gymnastics events are a lot of fun to watch, and you can pick up tips from the experts!

Competition layout

All of the events are on a stage that is 35 in. high. The equipment is spread out so that officials can see the gymnasts clearly. Judges award points based on how difficult a move is and how well it is performed.

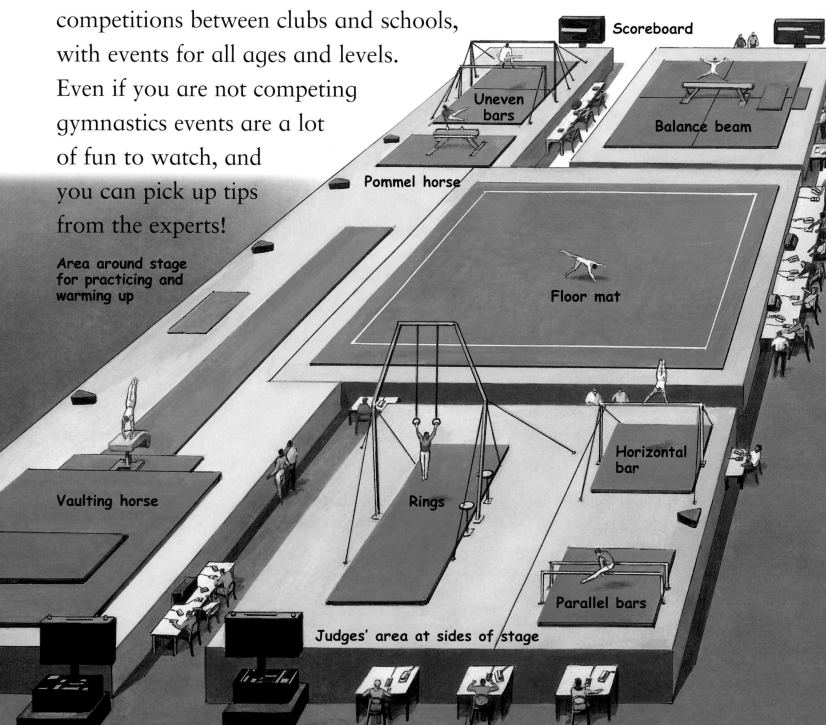

Area around stage for practicing and warming up

Scoreboard

Uneven bars

Balance beam

Pommel horse

Floor mat

Vaulting horse

Rings

Horizontal bar

Parallel bars

Judges' area at sides of stage

Glossary

apparatus Often called equipment. Hand apparatus is used in rhythmic gymnastics.

balance beam A narrow bar on which gymnasts perform different moves and balances.

balancing Holding the body still without falling over.

base In sports acrobatics the name for the gymnast who supports the weight of another.

chalk A fine white powder that gymnasts dust on their hands and feet to help them grip.

disciplines The different types of gymnastics that have developed over the years. These types include artistic gymnastics, rhythmic gymnastics, tumbling, trampolining, and sports acrobatics.

dismount The last move in a routine when the gymnast jumps off a balance beam or bar.

equipment The different types of apparatus used in gymnastics such as the balance beam or bar.

flexible Being able to bend the body easily.

grips Soft leather protectors worn on the hands—also known as handguards.

horse The padded equipment that gymnasts vault over.

mount To get on to a piece of equipment.

parallettes Pieces of equipment used for practicing handstands.

pike A V-shaped position made by bending the body at the hips.

posture The way that a person holds their body.

rhythmic gymnastics A type of gymnastics involving a floor routine set to music and hand apparatus such as a ribbon or ball.

routine A set of moves that are joined together.

somersault A full turn of the body that is performed in midair.

spotter A trained person who helps a gymnast practice their positions.

squat A position where a person crouches with their knees bent and their body weight on their feet.

straddle A position where the legs are stretched out wide apart.

tempo A type of exercise that is performed in sports acrobatics.

top In sports acrobatics the top is the gymnast who is balancing on another gymnast.

tumbling A discipline that involves somersaults and twists.

uneven bars A piece of equipment used by girls. It has two bars of different heights.

warm-up Gentle exercises that prepare the body for exercise.

Index

A
acrobatics 7, 10
acrobats 7, 10, 28, 29
arabesque 14
artistic gymnastics 4, 10, 24

B
back walkover 16–17
balance beam
4, 10, 11, 14,
15, 30, 31
balancing 14,
26, 28, 31
balls 23
bars 10, 11, 19
base 26, 27, 31
box split 11
bridge 10, 16
bull-leaping 6

C
chalk 19, 31
cheerleaders 29
Chinese State Circus 28
clubs 23
coach 8, 24
competitions 4, 8, 9,
20, 22, 26, 30
cross 18

D
dish 11, 16

E
equipment 11, 13, 30,
31
events 28, 30
exercising 9, 10

F
floor mat 4, 26, 30
floor work 10
foam mat 10

G
grips 19, 31
gym class 8

H
hand apparatus 5, 22, 23
handspring vault 20, 21
handstand 11, 14, 17, 18, 19, 20
headstands 14
hoops 22, 23, 28, 29
horizontal bars 5, 10, 30
human pyramid 28

J
judges 12, 27, 30
juggling 7
jumps 10, 13

L
leaps 10, 13, 20
leotards 9

O
Olympic Games 28,
30

P
parallel bars 4, 10,
17, 19, 30
parallettes 17, 31
pike jump 13, 31
pommel horse 4, 10,
20, 21, 30

R
rhythmic gymnastics 4, 5,
22, 31
ribbons 22, 23
rings 5, 9, 11, 17, 18, 19, 30
ropes 23

S
shoulder
balance 26
somersaults 6,
12, 19, 24, 25,
26, 31
sports acrobatics 4,
26
spotters 16, 25, 31
springboard 10, 20
stag leap 13

T
tempo 26, 31
top 26, 27, 31
training 9, 24
trampolining 4, 8,
13, 24, 25
triple balance 26
tumbling 4, 7, 10, 25,
26, 31
twists 17, 19, 25, 26

U
uneven bars 5, 10, 12, 19, 30

V
vault 4, 6, 7, 10, 11
vaulting horse 5, 20, 30
vaulting table 20

Y
Yurchenko full
twist 17